Hello, America!
U.S. Capitol

by Katherine Rawson

Bullfrog
Books

Ideas for Parents and Teachers

Bullfrog Books let children practice reading informational text at the earliest reading levels. Repetition, familiar words, and photo labels support early readers.

Before Reading

- Discuss the cover photo. What does it tell them?

- Look at the picture glossary together. Read and discuss the words.

Read the Book

- "Walk" through the book and look at the photos. Let the child ask questions. Point out the photo labels.

- Read the book to the child, or have him or her read independently.

After Reading

- Prompt the child to think more. Ask: What laws would you like to see passed at the U.S. Capitol?

Bullfrog Books are published by Jump!
5357 Penn Avenue South
Minneapolis, MN 55419
www.jumplibrary.com

Library of Congress Cataloging-in-Publication Data

Names: Rawson, Katherine, author.
Title: U.S. Capitol / by Katherine Rawson.
Description: Minneapolis, MN: Jump!, Inc., 2018.
Series: Hello, America! | "Bullfrog Books."
Includes index.
Identifiers: LCCN 2017027406 (print)
LCCN 2017027862 (ebook)
ISBN 9781624966620 (e-book)
ISBN 9781620318720 (hard cover: alk. paper)
Subjects: LCSH: United States Capitol (Washington, D.C.)—Juvenile literature.
Washington (D.C.) Buildings, structures, etc.
Juvenile literature.
Classification: LCC F204.C2 (ebook) | LCC F204.C2 R39 2018 (print) | DDC 975.3—dc23
LC record available at https://lccn.loc.gov/2017027406

Editor: Kirsten Chang
Book Designer: Molly Ballanger
Photo Researcher: Molly Ballanger

Photo Credits: Ferhat/Shutterstock, cover; M DOGAN/Shutterstock, 1; Songquan Deng/Shutterstock, 3; Annmarie Young/Shutterstock, 4 (flag); Chris Grill/Getty, 4; f11photo/Shutterstock, 5; Jerric Ramos/Shutterstock, 6–7, 23tl, 23br; Tetra Images/Getty, 8, 23mr; Rob Crandall/Shutterstock, 9; GraphicaArtis/Getty, 10–11; Onur ERSIN/Shutterstock, 12, 23bl; MPI/Stringer/Getty, 13; drnadig/iStock, 14–15; Kumar Sriskandan/Alamy, 16–17; Edwin Remsberg/SuperStock, 18–19, 23tr; Lopolo/Shutterstock, 20–21 (foreground); holbox/Shutterstock, 20–21 (background); Brendan Hoffman/Stringer/Getty, 22tl; Uwe Kazmaier/SuperStock, 22bl; The Washington Post/Getty, 22tr; Joe Ravi/Shutterstock, 22br; MasterQ/Shutterstock, 23ml; Keith McIntyre/Shutterstock, 24.

Printed in the United States of America at Corporate Graphics in North Mankato, Minnesota.

Table of Contents

Making Laws 4

Inside the Capitol 22

Picture Glossary 23

Index 24

To Learn More 24

Making Laws

We are in Washington, D.C.

Look! It's the U.S. Capitol!

It is big.

It is white.

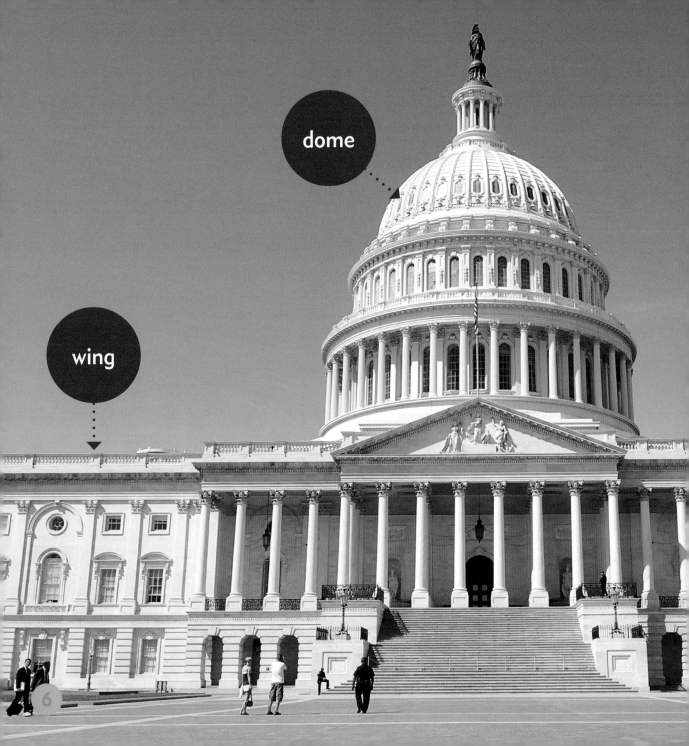

dome

wing

It has a dome.

It has two wings.

wing

People work here.
Voters elect them.

They make laws.
They try to make
our country better.

Many years ago, people came to this country.

They didn't want to be ruled by a king.

They wanted to rule themselves.

They made new laws.

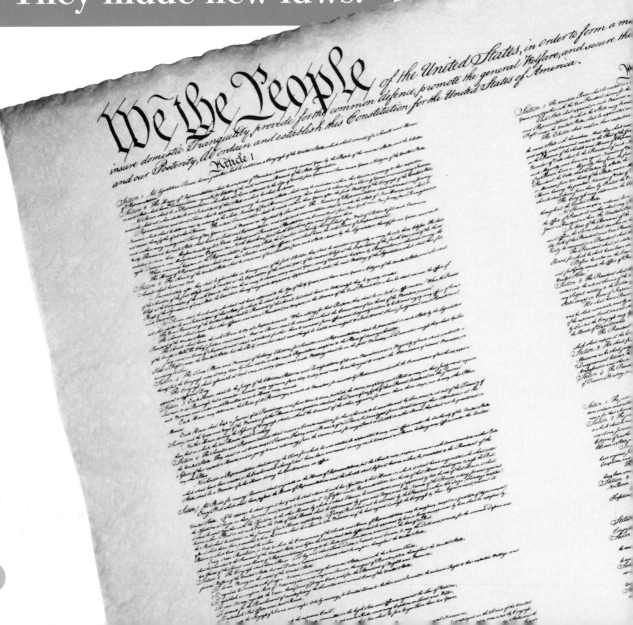

They built the Capitol.

Today, we can go inside.
Look up!
See the dome?
Wow! It is high!

See the art?

It shows our history.

See the statues?

They come from all the states.

JEFFERSON DAVIS

MISSISSIPPI

HENRY MOWER RICE

OREGON

REVEREND JASON LEE

FIRST MISSIONARY IN OREGON

19

We learned a lot at the Capitol!

Inside the Capitol

House Chamber
Representatives vote on laws here. It is in the south wing.

Senate Chamber
Senators vote on laws here. It is in the north wing.

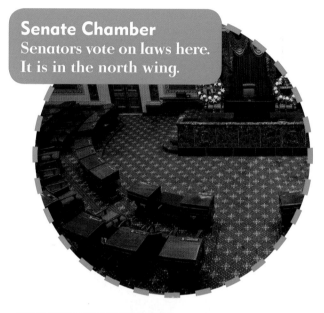

Rotunda
Ceremonies take place here.

Statuary Hall
These statues are of important people from different states.

Picture Glossary

dome
A large, round roof.

statues
Figures that represent people, usually made of stone or metal.

elect
To choose someone for an official position by voting.

voters
People who show support for a person or a plan by marking a ballot in an election.

laws
Rules that people must follow.

wings
Sections of a building that stick out from the main part.

Index

art 17

country 9, 11

dome 7, 14

elect 8

history 17

king 11

laws 9, 12

states 18

statues 18

voters 8

Washington, D.C. 4

wings 7

To Learn More

Learning more is as easy as 1, 2, 3.

1) Go to www.factsurfer.com

2) Enter "USCapitol" into the search box.

3) Click the "Surf" button to see a list of websites.

With factsurfer.com, finding more information is just a click away.